T0094654

The Politics of Knives

Jonathan Ball

Coach House Books, Toronto

Canada Council   Conseil des Arts    ONTARIO ARTS COUNCIL   Canadä
for the Arts   du Canada   CONSEIL DES ARTS DE L'ONTARIO

Published with the generous assistance of the Canada Council for
the Arts and the Ontario Arts Council. Coach House Books also
acknowledges the support of the Government of Canada through
the Canada Book Fund and the Government of Ontario through
the Ontario Book Publishing Tax Credit.

LIBRARY AND ARCHIVES CANADA CATALOGUING IN PUBLICATION

Ball, Jonathan, 1979-
    The politics of knives / Jonathan Ball.

Poems.
Issued also in an electronic format.
ISBN 978-1-55245-262-2

    I. Title.

PS8603.A55P65 2012   C811'.6   C2012-904675-2

The Politics of Knives is available as an ebook: ISBN 978 1 77056 320 9.

Contents

By this time Caesar found himself being attacked from every side, and as he glanced around to see if he could force a way through his attackers, he saw Brutus closing in upon him with his dagger drawn. At this he let go of Casca's hand which he had seized, muffled up his head in his robe, and yielded up his body to his murderers' blows. Then the conspirators flung themselves upon him with such a frenzy of violence, as they hacked away with their daggers, that they even wounded one another. Brutus received a stab in the hand as he tried to play his part in the slaughter, and every one of them was drenched in blood.

– Plutarch

My assassin brings me products I love.

– ryan fitzpatrick

The Process Proposed

First Manifesto

When she spoke, she did not speak
but with exhalation of wires.
Twelve awaited another.

When the process proposed.
Left her nothing but
time-limited amounts.

So iron sought skin.
And she said, 'I shall leak
oil and the wars for oil.'

Then a no-place gathering.
'If I must be a muse,' she said,
'then I will be terror.' And came.

Second Manifesto

A click as she shut
and then nothing opened
but into worlds of knives.

Seeking skin. She made
armour from glass and words
for glass and both shattered.

Letters in a heap. She said, 'Burn
my letters. Melt them and write
with their nothing, their no-ink.'

She made hyphens, made me use them.
Pulled brackets from her back. Saying:
'These in your throat and these around your neck.'

Third Manifesto

Where she touched, she bled.
She wore nothing but blades.
She did not believe in odds.

She exacted. Everything
had to be certain. Everything
had to balance on breaking.

I did not love her. She said,
'You must not love me.'
Tongue on teeth, chiselling.

When it was over.
In the final line:
her breath, caught.

In Vitro City

in vitro city, twenty-two lakes. in vitro city, drowning is a way of life. in vitro city, we hold hands holding heads under. in vitro city, nuclear devices recommissioned. in vitro city, a last resort. in vitro city, the walls are glass. in vitro city, all things are windows, so there are no windows.

in vitro city, glass is an industry. reamy, baroque, water-glass and other textures. ring mottles, fracture and streamers, drapery, granite and herringbone ripples. glass nipples. glass-making in the area. glass fibre for non-woven and textile applications. glass physics. glass service. glass museums. glass ceilings. glass ground.

in vitro city, how many live in furnished rooms? all hotels hold you, elevate penthouse to throne. you cannot separate. all these things that remain to be done.

in vitro city, protesters are not welcome. the riot police are not welcome. former members of the regime are not welcome. troops are not welcome. broken toys are not welcome. torn clothes are not welcome. perishables are not welcome. keys are not welcome. with this sex they are not welcome. in that skin they are not welcome. without money they are not welcome. you are not welcome.

in vitro city, lake salt suggests infinity. lamotrigine in the water supply. stability at what cost. the limestone parries its quarry, stone that screams.

in vitro city, the weather is always whether.

i awoke in vitro city and the world seemed a restless place. and wished for tomorrow. an image of the saviour near the clock, crowned by letters, he's not coming back. drone's battery dead and the site being bombed. they will close this account. the fish floating skyward. and why do i hurt. and where is this blood from. and what should i do. the question, marked.

in vitro city, bombs are being dropped. bombs on the market. at the box office. clustering. bombs in your father's land. by your father's hand. misnamed. erasers at the ends of penises.

in vitro city, what lives in this blind volume? there is no
god and we are its profits.

K. Enters the Castle

Only a total stranger could ask such a question. Are there control agencies? There are only control agencies.

In K.'s final, inevitable assault, he becomes a camera. In this way, K. enters the Castle.

This ending immanent in the story's first words, *no sign of the Castle hill, fog and darkness surrounded it, not even the faintest gleam of light suggested the large Castle.* Three times denied yet still seen. K. stands *a long time on the wooden bridge that leads from the main road to the village, gazing upward into the seeming emptiness.* That gaze this gaze, the camera's gaze, which sees even through darkness, through void, sees all a void. Tracking forward, zigzag down this mad road meant only for K. As a camera now, K. tracks forward, moves straight off this meaningless path, lens fixed on the spire in the distance. In the Castle's distance, where sits Count Westwest. K. aware of this sitting, but what gathers, masked there in that spire? Camera tracks its gaze forward, slow push through fog and darkness, to the gates to the gates, to the Castle nothing trammels K. now.

Camera moves through outer offices, their bustle and noise, racking forward, keeping all in focus, gliding quiet along makeshift rails, invisible to those scrambling for attention and those ignoring, checking books, past the sometimes passing of outdated messages, letters long dead. Past Klamm or the one who looks like Klamm, or no, looks nothing like Klamm, though he might be, the other a fake, past desire past hope, camera pushes through the wall and voices drop, the world recedes, its motions blur.

Then into the Castle, its emptiness, gone the bustle and noise, gone officials and scribes, cold stone spread empty. Not a noise, not a breeze sifting snow. Camera tracks through its streets, up cold stairways, down corridors. Nothing to capture, all the Castle abandoned, crumbling walls and cathedrals, strewn with papers. Lifeless papers spilled through the courtyard. Papers stacked along halls. Papers swept into corners. Under dust, stone, shelves tumbled haphazard, sheets crumpled and torn. K. takes no photographs, nothing warrants recording. No shadow moves, not a paper flits free.

So cold through the Castle, its papers and snow. Stillness ringed with officials and noise. They protect this stillness, these papers, the grey snow. All the Castle a wasteland. Camera pans to sky, cranes to survey the cold dead, papers strewn corpselike. Nothing worthy of note, a blankness below.

Camera clicks, whirs its lens, focus shifting over limp
papers, cracked stone. Seeks some trace of a system.
In that crazed spire? K.'s glass turns to its promise.
Creeps past papers, through stillness. Flagstones soaked
in silence, projector lit but the screen blank. Film unshot
still reeled in its dark.

But … control agencies. There are only control agencies. They sense this camera track silent, pan slow. Stand back from the pages, their long looping *K*s, power dormant. Not a shadow moves, no paper flits free.

Count Westwest, in his chambers, in the spire gleaming crazy, windows glinting out a reflected sun, recalls the wisdom of Augustine: *Illuc ergo venit ubi erat. He arrived where he already was.* At his desk, the final desk, head bowed, Westwest copies this sentence. But it is late evening when K. arrives, when the camera tracks here, my chair empty. In an empty room, at a desk, these empty words.

Psycho

Forget her name this bright longnecked bird. As the credits roll paramount. The letters break, the names in lines. Phoenix, Arizona. Friday, December the Eleventh. Two Forty-Three P.M. This autopsy through window her body lay legs long.

Half-naked on the bed in flesh she lies alone. A man in the room. Never did eat her lunch, black the bottle shadowed there. She leans in lean lips her bra, back, mouth. This the last time secretive. Rises face front buttoning. She will lick lick all the stamps, wants so what we want gone. To be alone with her in her white bra alone.

A headache a sister in Tucson fresh milk a not unhappy day. Her head with the money to the bank she heads now home. We'd spend weekends in her bed, her back bare bra black now, changed. She's changed, now dreamed into these arms.

Through the windshield now, pinned under glass. Looking out as we look he looks in, music, the pain of her face. In the headlights she sleeps by the road. Eyes seeking eyes there through glasses darkly. She should sleep to a motel soon, just to be safe.

In mirrors that car, then cars through the window. She steps out then around, the plates always looking sees paper eyes across the road. Just the car just a change. In the bathroom the mirror. Doubling desire.

Voices in her head, the road laying bare. The light in her eyes, in lips thin, closed, parted. Twitching she half-smiles what she's done. He will replace that money with her fine soft flesh.

Water falls thrumming, hard on motel. Vacancy wet, mother in window. She summons him with horns requests a room. What room shall he give, maybe two maybe three, two. She speaks, his hand falters. He likes her, in one puts her close.

Window open, mattress soft, the other side wall. She will eat with him eat but then mother comes down from the house. Oh what we'd give to dine. To trade places, invited. To her room to her room, then into the parlour instead.

The birds from his head spurt their wings. He's not hungry he'll watch while she eats, but much more than a hobby this she. Eats then speaks she sits still but she's running. While he talks of traps she steps into, on the wall the owl turns in its swoop.

Eyes studying, as if in a madhouse, she's sorry for saying she looks. As we look and look on, we all go mad sometimes. In us others desire, in our deaths we desire.

When she's gone we stay with him, through walls hear her moving. In holes place our eyes, her skin in black bra. Watching as he watches then home, and she writes. What she writes she then shreds. We don't read, but she writes.

But mother, we like her. She skins so beautiful, she showers for us clean.

She's dead but her eye still drains open. She's dead face
perfect, the floor screen. She's dead while the camera
keeps looking, as we stalk through this room mopped
so clean. Plastic, the car trunks her wet body. Knife-
chewed flesh that the swamp's swallowing. She's dead
and this letter for her, hurts our ears but they can't stop
talking. Now employed the detective finds fresh death.
Late-night snack, what long nights these have been. We
can rewatch that scene with no music. We can watch
and rewatch that same scene. She's dead as they search
through her cabin. She's dead all this black for blood
red. She's dead though he knew of no money. They
have their theories but she's dead.

All the mirrors, what shines in their glass. Dead hollows reflect outward, gaze. Eyes erased like our Norman erased. Why would we even harm a fly?

The Politics of Knives

████████████ not a small decision because those you choose should last a lifetime. They must be █████ and always ready, as if for backroom surgery. Providing economical, indispensable solutions to ██████████, proud to be the first choice of police and military professionals worldwide. Once the transfer is complete, you can enjoy the same █████ the stars employ.

████ covers his head. Every one warranted against defects in material and workmanship. Twenty-three, and all fury, but then solemn, enrobed in blood. ████████ is not recommended due to the risk of the blades snapping. A free trial is available for a limited time, after which your message will be returned to you in its true, inverted form.

Grasp the sheath well as you ███████████. Only in broken mirrors have the goals of assassins been realized. ██████████████, every shard its own currency and ████, it is easy with a quality stone.

The first ▮▮▮▮▮ focused on those who carry and use them. Acts often ▮▮▮▮▮▮▮ contrary to ▮▮▮▮▮▮▮ and so this poem, its contents and the cuts are provided on an 'as is' basis and no ▮▮▮▮▮▮▮▮▮▮▮ of any kind are explicit or implied.

638 attempts made on ██████████, exploding seashells considered and molluscs purchased before the idea set adrift, your tax dollars at work. ██████████████ more for your money with a set that will last a lifetime and tolerates no imitations. ████████████ more than justifies their expense and in any case what choice do you have? There is something to be said for ██████████████ and if you need to cut through ████ or a car door, don't laugh you will one day need to. Things you never considered, but those Things step into your footprints with great stealth.

And these are perfect for me. They have restored my ability to work. Although of limited use on normal missions, and to be carried only by someone willing to carry them. ███████ ████████████ trim the fat from the steak, for the leanest cuts possible. At heart it is a matter of personal preference, yet a duty for people of faith. It is the new Roman Empire, and will also fall. They demanded the release of members of ███████, but releasing those members was not an option. After the body was discovered, all were sentenced to ████████████, but this sentence terminated with ███████. If the company you work for is taken over, this could be the key to your survival.

That's one way to lose your audience, yelling 'as always to tyrants.' One thousand eyes flashed before ███ ██████████. Manufactured without ████████████, which makes them more hygienic, and using only the available light. The special one that resonates with you, which ████████████████, out of the hundreds you might see on the market. At dinner with his parents there was a knife she did not know how to use.

Carving, you botched the bird, a sure sign you need a new set, but if there is a code name then what is the code name? ████████████████████████████ ████████████████████████████ ████████████████████████████ ███████ put them to the test. If there is ████, then what ██████, and could there be errors ███████? Binary thinking leads to broken models. A slight separation, on this wire-fine edge. She was waving ██████ around and it made them all afraid.

Did they take ▮▮▮▮▮ home afterward, or let them fall clattering to the ground? ▮▮▮▮▮▮▮▮ washed in warm, soapy water, or an antibacterial bath, ▮▮▮▮▮▮▮▮, by ▮▮▮▮▮▮▮? Stamped ▮▮▮▮▮ thinner and lighter than forged. Made in ▮▮ now and ▮▮▮▮ and ▮▮▮▮▮, and in the last of the Empire's light and it made them all afraid.

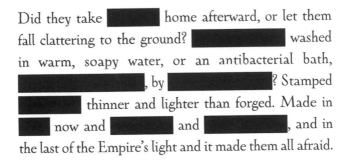

55

Many legends and many dubious. Was ███████████ poisoned or was it ██████████████? After that death made to die a second death, to prove to himself he was dead. Waking to the dream, to the angel known as God's assassin, and moving strong now, to ████████████████, because it comes calling our names.

███████████████████. Silverquick. ████████ drew the pistol and fired point blank, but the bullet failed to discharge, so ████████ drew a second pistol and fired point blank, but the bullet failed to discharge, and yet both times the gunshot was heard. An extended warranty provides peace of mind and when ████████ over skin featherlight, begs to bleed.

████████, and doomed to repeat. ████████.
What to do when the sheep elect wolves.

Then Wolves

when will you come when
all the world breathes out when
your passing such silence
the leaves gossip when

shattered songs with no chorus
children of delusion
of thorns brambles tangle
grey chattering things

WOLVES

counsel blindness
how sweetly die sparrows

let the angel of no lord
lost in the woods guide you

in a red hood with red hands
into these red halls

the berries are few now
rabbits and deer thin
every lover's axe murders
a child with no playthings

that straddles shadows
under trees that hang men
brittle forgotten stories
in books mouldering

WOLVES

seek skin supine
among sins swallow cake wine

let this bread be mould daily
let this hunger loose

songs howling break branches
through fur through torn chords

my love let them take me
to pasture to black burn
swords through my eyes letters
stillborn to ploughshares

knelt down on spun gold
riches in the next room
lacks lustre uncentred
webs encircling

WOLVES

tired unwind tears in
new skins buttress thorns

let me down where no safety
let the lord leave me terror

carry a false heart to
cover my footprints

when you sing you hold vowels
vow love though fear owns you
shape letters as flowers
take me elsewhere to horror

where shapeless things sharpen
lies loll on tongues dripping
tales unheard still written
in bones rotting marrow

WOLVES

wonder where they fit
their best teeth flash forward

let them not smell my passing
the forest floor over

leaves red fallen cover
the house of what lord

eaves running under
be careful of waiting
what lies at the end
of the forest this road

at the end of the sentence
no chorus repeating
what in the bed snaked
into skin to be shred

WOLVES

sent to the slaughter
how dark in this bedroom

let lamplight repeat me
mercy at my heels

repenting repeating
at this dessert drowned

where these letters tear
in wind the words whisper
this world whimpers reading
this are you what are you

lord what are you grant me
hells at my heels granted
eyes slit through what are you
why do you not run

WOLVES

dropping pretences
worn masks dot thin trails

let this forest end let
moonlight pen the ending

then tell me a story please
end it soon when

He Paints the Room Red

He paints the room red on the fourth day, perhaps to avoid symbolism. Until then, paint cans crouch in the southeast corner of the room, beside the thin desk, which the camera sees as the lower-right corner of the frame. Before anything else, he plants this camera.

As recording begins, he stands absent from this frame.

Striking our eyes, the room's picture window. He's opened the curtains and placed a small fan on the desk to approximate a breeze, ruffle their white frills.

Here, ambiguity nestles. Does he mean to approximate a breeze? Description bleeds into narrative, implies intention. But I do not mean to assign motivations to my subject, only offer this report.

In the main, I'll stick to what I know. He plants the camera and the window strikes the eye. It's midday and summer, the sun bright. Outside the open window, leaning left, a palm tree cuts the view. Its thick stalk explodes in a pinwheel, a leafy firework.

Beyond the tree, sky and ocean. Both a dazzle of white in the midday sun, overexposed – he's set the exposure and the focus to manual to avoid automatic image shifts as he enters the frame. He's turned off the microphone as well, so that his entire performance unfolds in silence. We neither see nor hear anything beyond this small, framed stage.

A writing desk slumps in the right of the frame, where the fan whirs. A clean red folding chair sits before the tidy white desk. Nothing else in view: just the window, its curtains, the tree, the desk, the fan, the chair, the cans, the bare walls.

I sit in this same hotel now, in another room. Near a bed (which would lie in the frame's left – he has removed his bed). There's a painting above it, an insipid landscape, another palm tree. The hotel contains no red chairs (mine is blue), so he must have brought that into the room.

If we could only see beyond the camera, behind it. But the camera never moves.

Nothing changes within the frame for eight hours. The fan turns, curtains swish. The palm outside sways in the intermittent breeze. He allows the camera to roll. In fact, he replaces the tape, which holds six hours of footage, but it's not clear when, nor how long he takes to change the tapes.

Whenever he does change them, he minimizes the disturbance, so that it seems no time has passed, nothing has changed. Although we know, after the fact, that he stayed in the hotel for a week, and that he painted the room red on the fourth day. Altogether, the performance ranges over twelve tapes, seventy-two hours. It's always bright, overexposed. Always the midday sun.

When he enters the frame, carrying the typewriter, the shock of his arrival brings with it some brutality. He lopes through the room, from frame left to the desk on the right, with the violent stride of a wolf. His back to the camera as he moves to the desk.

All the energy of the film gathers around him. We've been waiting. Everything in the room, even the light, seems turned to him, to his overexposed skin.

In a buttoned shirt, wine-red, like the chair. Like the cans of unopened paint. Bright nightmares. Black dress pants, a matching belt, neat black shoes. Head shaved clean. Facing the wall.

He always enters from the left, exits on the right. Circling back behind the camera. When he enters again, he carries a stack of paper. Settles down to the typewriter, his back to us, face always turned away. He starts to type.

He types for thirty-six hours. Getting up to change tapes, replenish paper. With his body in the way, we cannot see what he types. The paper, like the sky, like his skin – overexposed.

He writes and we watch him write, and I write this. The papers pile up.

Whatever he writes flows out of him. Never does he stop and search for words. If indeed what he types contains words. If he's written anything, if it's not all an act.

When he finishes typing, he paints the room red. He begins in the area surrounding the paint cans. He paints the corner, the floor, both walls. He paints the desk. He paints the typewriter. He paints the cans themselves. Large goopy swipes. He uses a thick horsehair brush, slathers paint everywhere. By the end even the handle of the brush drips red. The only thing he does not paint over are the papers themselves.

This painting takes up twenty-four hours of tape, of this endless day. The entire frame, except for the white papers, soaked in red. The last thing he paints is the window. Removes the curtains, dips them into the buckets, hangs them again. Paint streams down their lengths like fresh blood. He then passes the brush over the glass. A thin coat to cover the window. So the room's light tints red, and the papers turn red in that light.

He leaves the frame again, for a moment. Through all this we never see his face. The papers still lie on the table, this book he's written, or pretended to write.

He returns naked, body shaved clean, with a matchbox and a small red tin. Opens the tin and pours out the liquid, over the book. Strikes a match. Puts the pages to its flame.

The flame bursts, what he's poured must be gasoline. The rest trickles down over his head. He sets his dripping hand down on the burning book.

Soon the whole room is ablaze. The heat shatters the window. There are four hours left on this last tape. For hours in his created world, we watch our faceless author burn.

I do not know his reasons. I don't understand any of this. You'll object. You'll say: he's your character. You'll say: you wrote him, we read this, we know.

You will blame me, and maybe you should. You will say: where is our story? But you watched him. As he burnt it. And you did nothing, just like me.

I'm in a hotel, far from home. A palm tree sways outside the window. Does the palm tree understand? It was here the whole time too.

To Begin

This is not a confession. He came across the water. Light broke the lake. The stone shore would not take his footprints. He raised arms. The fish sang. A bird took the sky and brought it home to weave into its nest. Impossible, yet there. You must believe.

He thought he recognized the song. A true story. Once upon a time, a woman smelled of apples. Her children did not move. A knock at the door, which spilled toward the fist.

When she left, he followed. She led him down unwritten alleyways, into desperation. Two families, and they were at war.

Blood dripped, stars fell. The sea scarred. The sun retreated. Rain more constant than he had ever been. Someone's always crying. The lake hissed, flaming. The child dove into the water. She curled tight so as not to scream, or he would find her.

Somewhere, dogs bayed. That night, the wind took down trees. The boat turned. Nowhere safe. The clouds opened, swallowed, closed. They were drinking when it happened. She had never been in love. The knife slipped. Her heart fell. In this beginning darkness, before fire.

The betrayal so sudden she could not react. The storm built them a new, cleaner world.

By the time he understood, it was too late. Drowned clutching at fish, reaching out for life. He dropped the glass and awoke. She did not know where she was, where she had been.

He knew every inch of the room, knew it better than her. That year the hotel burned down. The forest sighed. Sickness stole eyes. The cat wanted milk, a page turned.

Outside, secrets, wind whispered. The days in rows, their stunted growth. The leaves began to turn into something new. In the house across the street, light.

The walls glass, and the night as well. Growing into infernos. He slipped the hammer from his pocket. Certain of nothing now.

.

Something rose: the hated moon. The mist dissolved what it did not need. She cried. Outside was impossible.

She looked him over. In secret places, worlds slip into one another. The garden choked beneath ancient neglect. Shots rang, and the phone died. The house remained empty for a long, long time.

Every story is true, somewhere. Walls falling to dust. Gates bending. The land suffering, silent and cold. The light that left them has taken the child. Something must happen soon.

She runs, out of options. He gasps, losing air. Someone lights a match. A promise readies to break. I don't know what to say, where to begin. We sit together in this burned room, waiting.

That Most Terrible of Dogs

Waiting. Waiting to catch the drift. Waiting
for something empirical and wise. Waiting for
the ration of rainwater to decrease and the
runoff to increase, for the river's end in silt
and toil. Waiting to be impressed with all said.
Waiting to know who is speaking at all times.
Waiting while the pages turn. Waiting to find
out it's really great and since submitting my life
has changed. Waiting in the material world.
Waiting for all that exists in this cave of forms
to be perfect. Waiting for the collision of two
plates to produce deadly forces. Waiting for
triggers and hairy delirium. Waiting for denial
and magpies. Waiting to be conversant in veal.
Waiting for acrimony used as a literary device.
Waiting to stagger antagonistically toward an
ejection. Waiting for my car to humanize and
tap reserves. Waiting for less final solutions.
Waiting for warlords to decide. Waiting for
atrocity, the exhibition begun. Waiting to pole
vault over bookmakers. Waiting for compen-
sation. Waiting for the files. Waiting in the
rain, lined pockets for waterproofing. Waiting
for terroristic improvements. Waiting for a

boost to become underrated. Waiting to adopt a panicky creed. Waiting for the theatre of the tabloid. Waiting for phrasing with nitrogen. Waiting to teem. Waiting to cleverly make contact with the myth. Waiting to thwart haste, to recur. Waiting to effectively use the existing infrastructure in the most efficient of possible manners. Waiting to see the real war while the public seethes national isms. Waiting to become more involved in these stories. Waiting to be whatever I want to be, but first I must be willing to work. Waiting for a skin unlike others. Waiting for the empire to mount its tenants, and soon after market my resilience. Waiting to thrive on the wiretaps. Waiting to glow and decay. Waiting for the violence of the megaton. Waiting for inspiration, surreal and corrosive. Waiting to be involved in a third-rate gallery love affair. Waiting for resistance, bleeding hunger strikes. Waiting for your sneaking blush to grey. Waiting for new moderns, in the voting booth dumb. Waiting for provisions to show me the way. Waiting until they can quantify the results. Waiting to love the aggravation and drudgery. Waiting to test my hypothesis, for the best man to become a heavenly windbreaker. Waiting to speak with the creator of society and grapefruit. Waiting for my soup, torrent pummelling the patio. Waiting to embarrass those bourbon federalists. Waiting for the adultery to hemorrhage. Waiting for the period that comes after the outboard motor. Waiting while, over yonder, a credit card gleams. Waiting with crossed thighs for a few posthumous guarantees. Waiting to fasten my principles to cynical schemes. Waiting with the impartiality of a counterfeiter. Waiting for my luck to bygone. Waiting, glorious in insomnia. Waiting for the anniversary of the fetus overcome. Waiting for a series of vicious courtships. Waiting, boastful and rectal, quoting panhandlers. Waiting for the affirmative, to tar the feathers, short circuits, deploy nausea. Waiting to resign over corruption charges, pending one emptied trust fund per day. Waiting for rheumatism, lumbago and other slash somesuch complaints. Waiting, hands on my guns, for the plain fact that it was my heart. Waiting with my pennants for eternity. Waiting to discover the full potential of my lawn. Waiting for the delish delisting of all of these saccharin products. Waiting with the other parishioners for the generalized entity. Waiting to take the shortcut, the barrel. Waiting to pervert it all.

Waiting for exoneration, alleviation, disloca-
tion, to be rephrased. Waiting for my genera-
tion to generate. Waiting for nourishment, thus
nonchalantly, as the king cheetah stripe.
Waiting to increase my vocabulary with an
adventure safari, in homeroom where twelve
dead monkeys hang. Waiting to appeal to the
working-class literati. Waiting, succinct. Wait-
ing to swelter and tire. Waiting to address the
increasing gap between rich and poor, the huge
international debt, and to redesign those now
responsible. Waiting for actions and events
happening around me to hurtle beyond my
control. Waiting for what you want of this jade.
Waiting in a non-violence quandary. Waiting
to be misread. Waiting for the intense retail
reality of the hornet shopkeeper buzzing
around its pie charts. Waiting in studied irrev-
erence. Waiting to deflect openness, deforest
anarchy. Waiting to nurture the apolitical.
Waiting for the athletes to seem tastier.
Waiting as an enraged post-artisan. Waiting
incongruous with the voyage. Waiting to
steamroll over the palaeontology of ice. Wait-
ing to condense after a series of trials. Waiting,
confident in my ascetic. Waiting and indulging
my inner sociopath. Waiting on the on-ramp to

extinction. Waiting for the next step of this program, when the ratings push us through the screen. Waiting, shall we say, with your eyes. Waiting drunk and unsure of my spoon. Waiting in the jaws of Cerberus, that most terrible of dogs.

Acknowledgments

Thanks to Mandy Heyens for her understanding and support. Thanks to Jessie Taylor, who keeps me on my toes. Thanks also to the rest of my family, and to friends who have gone unmentioned, for various kindnesses.

Thanks to Jean-Luc Beaudry, derek beaulieu, Erin Bockstael, Christian Bök, Natalee Caple, Emily Carr, G. M. B. Chomichuk, Dennis Cooley, Chris Ewart, kevin mcpherson eckhoff, Jon Paul Fiorentino, ryan fitzpatrick, Ariel Gordon, Kaylen Hann, Catherine Hunter, Sandy Lam, Jeremy Leipert, Colin Martin, Suzette Mayr, Maurice Mierau, Jay MillAr, David Navratil, Mike Roberson, William Neil Scott, Patrick Short, Colin Smith, John Toone, Natalie Zina Walschots, Lindsey Wiebe and Caleb Zimmerman for good times, inspiration, many meals, great discussions and valuable feedback.

'The Process Proposed' was written as a perversion of the traditional invocation of the muse, and published as a chapbook by my own press, The Martian Press. Parts of 'In Vitro City' were published in *NōD* and *Phantom Drift*. 'The Politics of Knives' was published in *dANDelion*. 'Then Wolves' was published by Book-Thug in a far different form, as the chapbook *wolves (lone.ly)*. 'To Begin' was published as a chapbook by Nº Press. 'That Most Terrible of Dogs' was published in *Matrix* and *The Capilano Review*. The present forms of these works could not have evolved without passing through these prior incarnations.

The epigraph from Plutarch is taken from *Makers of Rome* (*Penguin*, 1965), translated by Ian Scott-Kilvert. The epigraph from ryan fitzpatrick is taken from the poem 'Because You're the Comic Relief' in the book *Fake Math* (Snare, 2007). The question 'how many … live in furnished rooms' was posed by Leonard

Cohen in the poem 'I Wonder How Many People in This City' from *The Spice-Box of Earth* (McClelland & Stewart, 1961). 'In Vitro City' concludes with two détournements of phrases from, respectively, Jorge Luis Borges's 'The Total Library' from *Selected Non-Fictions* (Viking, 1999) and Cormac McCarthy's *The Road* (Knopf, 2006). 'K. Enters the Castle' is indebted to Mark Harman's translation of Franz Kafka's *The Castle* (Schocken, 1998), from which the quotations on page 23 and 25 are drawn. The Latin quotation from Augustine is drawn from *Postmodernist Fiction* by Brian McHale (Metheun, 1987), though this translation and its failures are my own.

Thanks to everyone at Coach House Books: to Kevin Connolly and Alana Wilcox, for their outstanding editorial superpowers, to Evan Munday for his stunning ability to promote even me, to Leigh Nash for much work behind the scenes, and to Stan Bevington for making all possible.

Thank you, goodnight.

About the Author

Jonathan Ball, Ph.D., teaches English, film and writing at the University of Manitoba and the University of Winnipeg. He is the author of *Ex Machina* (BookThug, 2009) and *Clockfire* (Coach House Books, 2010), which was shortlisted for a Manitoba Book Award. *Ex Machina* considers the relationship between humans, books and machines, and *Clockfire* contains seventy-seven plays that would be impossible to produce. Like *The Politics of Knives*, these books were published under Creative Commons licences, so you can remix their contents. Jonathan also directed the short films *Spoony B* and *Opening Band*. Visit Jonathan online at www.jonathanball.com or @jonathanballcom.

Typeset in Oneleigh, designed in 1999 by Toronto's Nick Shinn. Oneleigh has obvious roots in traditional roman serifed types, however this face takes on an eccentric character of its own due to its unique forms and loose, almost hand-drawn appearance in both display and text settings, making it very lively on the page.

Printed in July 2012 at the old Coach House on bpNichol Lane in Toronto, Ontario, on Zephyr Antique Laid paper, which was manufactured, acid-free, in Saint-Jérôme, Quebec, from second-growth forests. This book was printed with vegetable-based ink on a 1965 Heidelberg KORD offset litho press. Its pages were folded on a Baumfolder, gathered by hand, bound on a Sulby Auto-Minabinda and trimmed on a Polar single-knife cutter.

Edited by Kevin Connolly
Designed by Alana Wilcox
Author photo by Mandy Heyens
Cover photo, *Stolen Summer*, by Robert and Shana
    ParkeHarrison, courtesy of the artists

Coach House Books
80 bpNichol Lane
Toronto ON M5S 3J4
Canada

416 979 2217
800 367 6360

mail@chbooks.com
www.chbooks.com